Natural Remedies

Natural Remedies

Plant Cures

Manisha Jain

Rupa & Co

Published in 2002 by
Rupa . Co
7/16, Ansari Road, Daryaganj
New Delhi 110 002

Sales Centres:
Allahabad Bangalore Chandigarh Chennai
Dehradun Hyderabad Jaipur Kathmandu
Kolkata Ludhiana Mumbai Pune

ISBN: 81-7167-788-6

Cover & Book Design by
Arrt Creations
45 Nehru Apts, Kalkaji, New Delhi 110 019

Printed in India by
Gopsons Paper Ltd
A-14 Sector 60
Noida 201 301

Contents

Natural Remedies

The significance of herbs and plants for the health and well-being of human beings has been stressed since the olden days. In fact the knowledge and use of herbs have originated from ancient India and the world is indebted to it for the same. Ancient sages, thinkers and doctors have said that the best way to have good health and peace of mind is by going back to Nature and utilising its rich bounty of herbs and plants.

"Saatwik" food, that is, a vegetarian diet consisting of a simple combination of fruit, vegetables, cereals and flour, has for long been recommended for a sound mind in a sound body.

Your very own kitchen and garden are the richest sources of good health, beauty and freedom from illness. Common plants like mint, ginger and coriander,

can send irksome diseases flying out of the window. Herbs which are easily available, can also become the delight of the modern woman, who wants to look attractive while efficiently going about her duties. Some of these are excellent cures for beauty problems. They only have to be mixed properly, in the right proportions. Inexpensive face masks and body washes can be made quickly. They are easy on the wallet and save needless expenses at the local beautician or the chemist shops.

Fresh sauces, soups and marmalades can be made at home. You can get both purity and nourishment without spending much money.

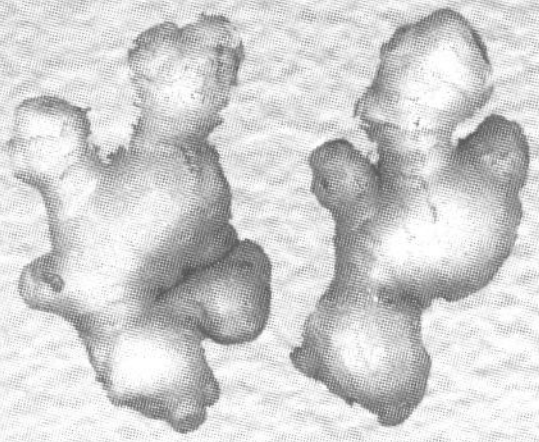

Ginger

Highly recommended by doctors throughout the year because of its antiseptic and healing nature. It is a popular ingredient in pickles and salads. It can be had raw or cooked. It acts as a digestive. It is used while cooking vegetables like cauliflower, black gram and lentils as it reduces flatulence. It cures respiratory disorders, fatigue and dizziness. It is refreshing and has a cooling effect on the body. It increases blood circulation and cures joint pains. It is recommended for cold, nausea, headache and vertigo.

- Ginger soda. Take 250 gm ginger, the juice of two lemons, salt and sugar according to taste. Mix in a blender. Strain out the juice and fill in a bottle. The concentrate can be mixed with fresh soda or water. It is refreshing and gives instant energy.

- Finely slice a few pieces of ginger stem. Slit fresh, green chillies and add to the ginger along with salt and vinegar. Can be eaten as a salad or preserved as a pickle.

Turmeric

Antiseptic in nature and is well-known for healing broken bones and sprains. Cures laziness, lassitude and enhances alertness. It aids digestion and improves eyesight. Is an excellent blood purifier and an essential cosmetic aid. In fact, a bride's vanity case is considered incomplete without "haldi uptan". Used to cure insomnia, sinusitis, cough and respiratory diseases.

Local application of "haldi" is recommended for sprains and injuries. Helps tired eyes.

- Take 10 gm of turmeric and boil in 20 ml water. Cool. Take a muslin cloth and soak in the haldi water. Apply on tired and irritated eyes. Can sprinkle the turmeric water on the eyes.

- A paste of turmeric powder and warm mustard oil can be applied locally on swellings and sprained joints. It reduces inflammation and soothes pain. In fact, for healing fractured bones, drink hot milk mixed with turmeric powder over a considerable period of time. It is a natural healing agent.

Neem

This herb contains a high content of protein, calcium, vitamin A and neem. The bark of neem is commonly used as "datun" to clean teeth and tongue. Neem leaves are antiseptic. They prevent rotting by moths and worms and can be used to line woollens and silk clothes in trunks and cupboards. It is good for the skin and can be applied on rashes, boils and pimples. It is antiseptic. Good for swollen eyes, itchy skin and burns.

- Take 50 gms of neem leaves and put in 250 gm boiling mustard oil. Cook for a few minutes. Cool and run through a sieve. Store in a bottle. Can be applied on wounds and burns.
- Neem juice can be mixed with warm water and salt for gargling.
- Crush a few neem leaves and mix in half a cup of water. Drink this mixture to stop vomiting.

Sugarcane

It is nicknamed the "blood bank" of the human body. Sugarcane contains all the ingredients needed for the nourishment of the body. It improves blood circulation and increases the red blood corpuscles in the blood. It brings a shine to the teeth and complexion. Prevents tooth decay and cold. It energises the body. Cures jaundice and heart disease.

- Use sugarcane juice to sweeten *kheer*. It aids in digestion and purification of the blood.
- Sugarcane juice should be given regularly to people who have lost blood due to injuries.
- Jaggery, made from sugarcane juice is a healthy substitute for sugar in tea and coffee.

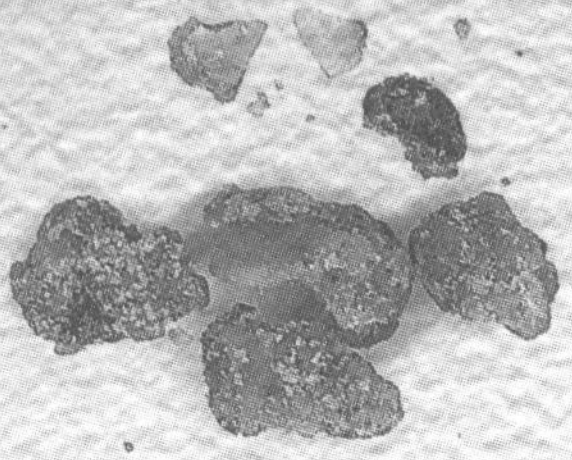

Asofoetida

Asofoetida *(heeng)* is quite an expensive herb but nevertheless it is an important ingredient for gravies, curries and pickles. It adds a unique, tangy flavour to vegetables and rice dishes. Pickles, especially mango pickle, are incomplete without being seasoned with this delicious herb.

Asofoetida is an excellent digestive. A few grains in any gravy, chutney or soup, ensures quick digestion of the food. It rids the system of gas and flatulence. It cleanses the digestive system. It is good for joint pains and should be taken with warm water early in the morning. It is highly recommended during cold, cough and sinusitis.

- *Churan* made by mixing *heeng*, *jeera*, salt and sugar, is very good for the stomach. It cures giddiness and nausea.

- Add ample portions of asofoetida while preparing mango and lemon pickle. It acts as a natural preservative and also enriches the taste.

Pomegranate Seed

Anardana, as it is popularly called, contains Vitamin A and C. It aids digestion and has a settling effect on the stomach.

Powdered *anardana* is a popular spice in Indian dishes. It is mixed in chutneys and pickles. Because of its sour taste, it is used to flavour savouries and vegetable gravies.

- It cures headaches and nausea. It is good for acidity and flatulence.
- *Anardana* churan is very effective in curing ailments related to the stomach. It settles a queasy stomach almost instantly.
- Its sour taste helps remove nausea, gas and flatulence.

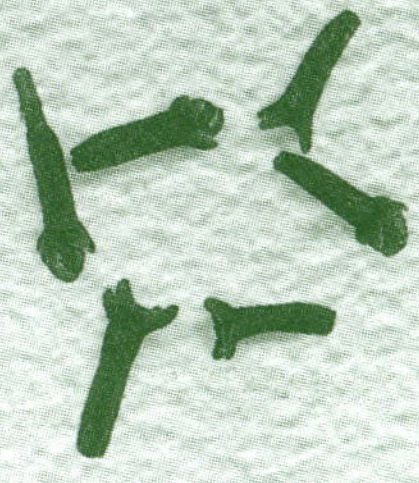

Clove

Clove *(laung)* is an expensive spice. It is highly valued for its medicinal value. It is excellent for chest congestion, cold and cough. A few cloves mixed in tea water, is a good remedy for headaches. Clove oil is antiseptic in nature and brings relief to pain in teeth and gums. It cures stomach cramps and digestion problems. It is used as a condiment to flavour tomato ketchup and soups.

It is generally added to lend a rich taste to vegetable gravies.

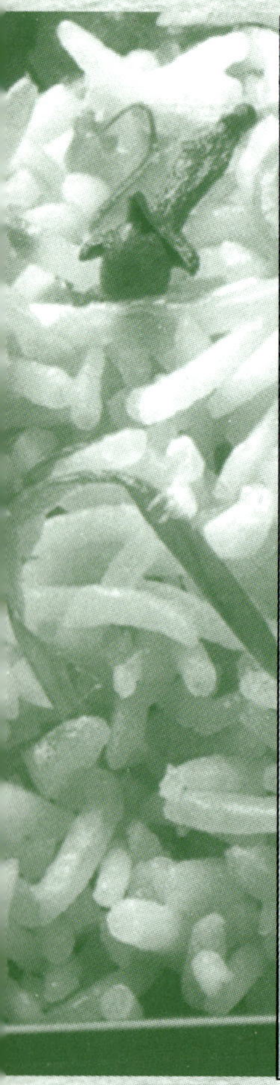

- Take a few pieces of clove and wrap in a thin, muslin cloth. Tie the mouth with a thread, Sprinkle a few drops of water on this small bag. Suspend this bag near the rim of the soup or vegetable you are cooking. This will lend a pleasing, clove flavour to the dish.

- Add clove while cooking halwa, kheer and other sweet dishes.

- Clove makes a good beauty aid. It clears pimples and blemishes. Crush a few cloves and mix with rose water. Apply the paste thinly over face and let dry. Splash cold water and pat dry. Regular use will clear the skin and also tone it up.

Cardamom

Cardamom or *elaichi* is considered to be the queen of spices. A popular ingredient in Indian sweets, vegetables and rice dishes, elaichi is also added to flavour tea. Grandmothers prescribed tea, laced with clove and cardamom, for preventing coughs and colds during the winter months. Cardamom guards against chest congestion and lends warmth to the body. It also adds a pleasant aroma to tea.

It is recommended for irritability and restlessness of temper. It cures headaches and improves blood circulation.

- Cardamom is generously used in rice biryani and pulao.

- Boil two cardamoms in a cup of water. Add a spoon of honey. Drink it just before going to bed. Clears sinuses and relieves chest congestion.

Cinnamon

Cinnamon *(dalcheeni)* is another very expensive herb. It, in a way, completes the family of clove and cardamom. The three are generally ground and kept aside to mix in tea water before boiling. Cinnamon cures coughs, colds and respiratory disorders. It is good for the stomach but should not be had in excess in summer.

It brings relief to gastric disorders and queasy stomachs. It has a strong and pungent smell.

- A small cinnamon stick can be put in the teapot while the tea is brewing. If you want a stronger flavour, then grind and mix a pinch of the cinnamon powder while the water is boiling.

- Cinnamon powder can also be mixed with hot milk. It is good to drink this just before going to bed. It gives warmth and also relaxes the body. An excellent prelude to a soothing, restful sleep.

Mint

Mint or *pudina* is rich in iron, protein, Vitamin A and B. It is very good for strengthening the eyes. It improves body resistance and the haemoglobin level in the blood. It is a good cure for anaemia, night blindness, weak eyes and body weakness.
Mint is widely used in making chutneys and *raitas*. It is good for the stomach and helps digestion. It is good for lowering cholestrol.

- Mint is an essential ingredient in mouth fresheners and chewing gum. It is also used in toothpaste and mouth washes.

- Decorate your salad bowl with a few leaves of fresh mint. Chop mint leaves finely and add to *raita*, making it both tasty and nutritious.

Tulsi

This herb is considered to be highly auspicious. It is believed that placing it in the centre of the courtyard brings good luck and prosperity in the household. Watering a tulsi plant everyday has an energizing and healing effect. It cures negative attitude.

Tulsi improves blood circulation, throat infection and cures skin diseases. It also cools the temper considerably and gives mental strength and concentration. It is refreshing to add tulsi leaves to your bathwater.

- Add a few teaspoons of tulsi juice to pulao and rice for extra flavouring.

- Add a few leaves of tulsi while boiling tea leaves. Cures bad throat and cough.

- Apply cottonwool soaked in tulsi water over tired eyes. Removes itching and also cleans the eyes in the process.

Amla

Amla is the richest source of natural Vitamin C. It also contains Vitamin A and E. It is a highly recommended fruit for students as it improves eyesight and increases alertness. Good for healthy bones, gums and teeth.

- Amla pickle: Slit amlas. Make a thick syrup of sugar. Add salt, vinegar and citric acid to taste. Take a broad-mouthed glass jar and put the amlas in it. Pour the syrup on top and seal the lid tightly. Let it stand in the sun for 2–3 days before use.

- Amla juice is very refreshing and can be had with salt or sugar according to taste.

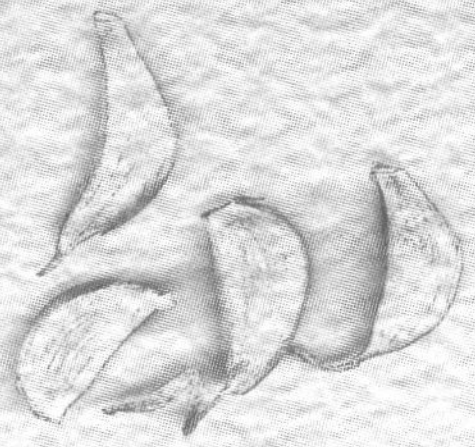

Garlic

This strong-smelling herb is rich in Vitamin A, C and Vitamin B complex. It also contains Vitamin E, iron, magnesium, phosphorus and potassium. This versatile herb is widely used as a medicine. It is used by the rich and the poor alike to keep away diseases and evil spirits.

It is used to flavour butter, cheese, vinegar, dried seasoning and salad dressings. Used widely while preparing soups and main dishes.

It performs the important task of rejuvenating body cells and repairing them. It is recommended for back and joint pains, tuberculosis and asthma. The fresher the garlic, the better it works.

- It lowers blood cholestrol, cleanses the stomach and cures gastric disorders.

- Garlic intake is recommended for whooping cough, lead poisoning and some carcinoma.

- It controls mild diabetes and appendicitis.

- Crush a few cloves of garlic to make a paste. Apply on swelling or painful joints. This relieves the pain quickly.

- A few cloves of garlic taken with a glass of warm water, first thing in the morning, is good for acidity and joint pains.

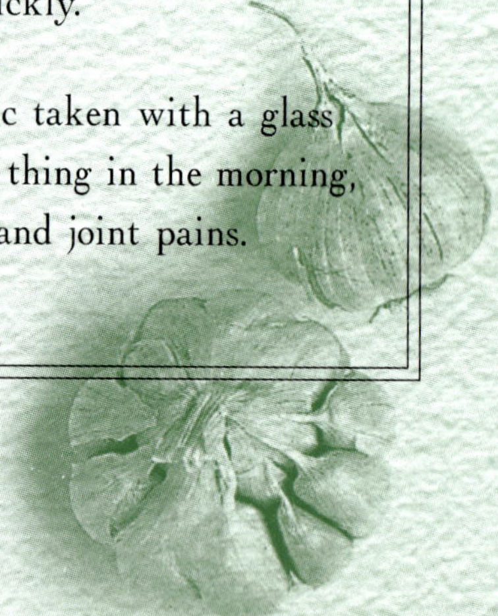

Oregano

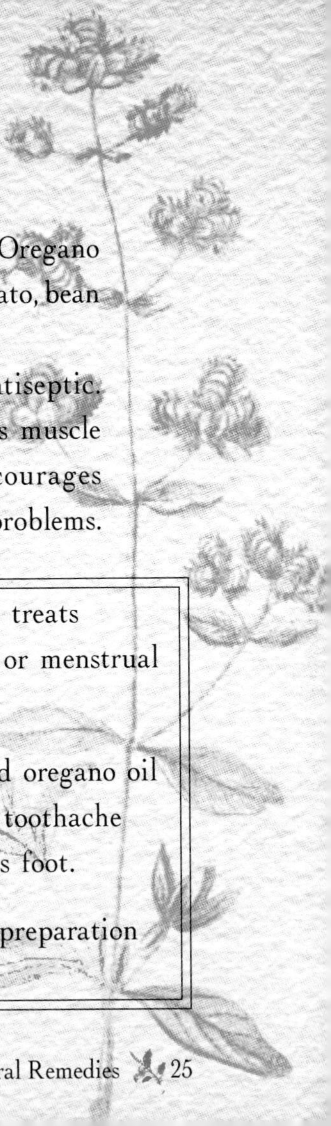

This is a popular seasoning herb. Oregano often accompanies basil in cheese, tomato, bean dishes and pizzas.

It is an expectorant and an antiseptic. Oregano improves digestion, reduces muscle spasms and inflammation. It encourages menstruation and helps respiratory problems.

- Oregano is a weak sedative and treats nervous headaches, irritability or menstrual cramps.
- It kills intestinal worms. Diluted oregano oil can be rubbed on insect bites, toothache and skin fungi such as athlete's foot.
- Oregano leaves are used in the preparation of dyes.

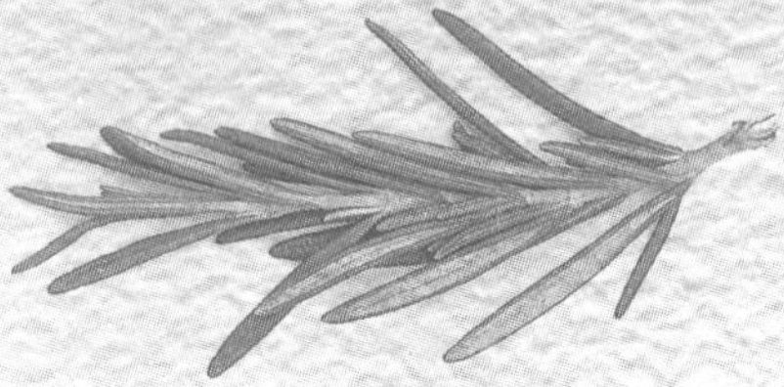

Rosemary

This is a tall, stout shrub with pale, blue flowers. Rosemary, because of these ornamental, stately flowers, is used as a decoration herb.

It is a powerful food preservative and an anti-oxidant. Rosemary increases circulation and reduces headaches. It fights bacterial and fungal infections. It strengthens fragile blood vessels. It stimulates digestion, liver, intestinal tract and the gall bladder. It inhibits the formation of kidney and bladder stones.

- Rosemary ointments can be rubbed for nerve and rheumatic pains and for heart problems.

- Rosemary extract is ideal to improve poor circulation.

- It makes an antiseptic gargle for sore throats and gum problems.

- Rosemarinic acid is a good treatment for septic shock.

- Rosemary should be added to baths and liniments to stimulate and warm the skin and relax museles.

- It is used in eau de cologne, hair shampoos and conditioners as it decreases dandruff. It is also used to flavour toothpastes.

Jasmine

This herb has beautiful, white flowers which exude a lovely fragrance. The fragrance increases at night and the flowers continue to have a lovely scent for days after being picked.

Jasmine flowers are popularly used to make *gajra* to adorn hair. The plant looks particularly attractive if grown on a trellis. They are considered to be auspicious and are used for religious occasions. They are also offered to gods and goddesses during traditional puja.

Jasmine can be used to add a light, perfumed flavour to tea and other beverages. It clears the blood of impurities.

- A syrup made of jasmine flowers is very good for curing cough and cold.
- Chewing of jasmine leaves is good for curing mouth ulcers.
- Make leaf-tea to rinse sore eyes and wounds.
- Headaches and insomnia are relieved with tea made from the root of jasmine.
- Jasmine makes a very popular *attar*. It is a cosmetic oil used widely in perfumes.
- Jasmine is good for skins that are hot, dry and overly sensitive.

Bay

This is a stout tree with dark purple to black berries. Bay leaves *(tejpatta)* are commonly used in soups, stews and bean dishes. It releases its flavour for hours. It is commonly used as a pickling spice.

Bay has a cool fragrance and is used in men's colognes and scents. Its black berries and leaves can be used to calm queasy stomachs.

Bay is antiseptic in nature. In olden times, bay leaves were used to improve the memory and cure headaches.

Greek priestesses at ancient Delphi sat over fumes of what were probably burning bay leaves to inspire prophetic visions.

- A paste of bay leaves and honey is effective for removing blemishes.
- Bay helps cure skin problems and bruises.

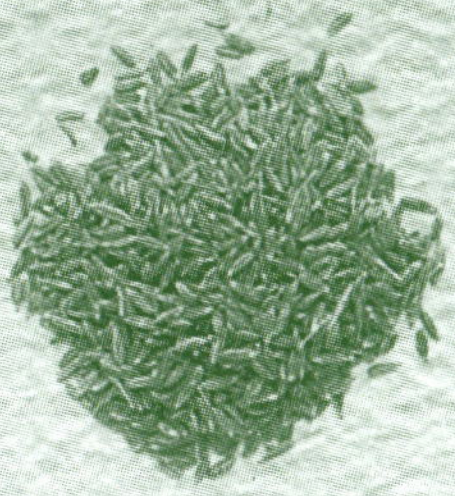

Cumin

Cumin seeds *(jeera)* form an integral part of any kitchen's spice rack *(masala daani)*. They are used to flavour curries, curds and chutneys. It is a popular ingredient in *churan* because of its digestive properties. It aids digestion and reduces flatulence.

It also checks obesity. Cumin is used to treat liver and urinary problems. It cures diarrhoea.

- Cumin powder serves as an excellent additive in raitas and chutneys. Take about 100 gms of cumin seeds and roast for a few minutes on a red-hot tawa. Keep tossing till they turn blackish-brown. Cool and grind in a mixer. Store in a jar.

- Grind equal quantities of cumin seeds and dry ginger. Mix salt, sugar and water to make a paste. Roll into small balls. Store this churan into a small plastic or glass bottle.

Lavender

This fragrant, pathway hedge contains essential oils, eucalyptol and linalol. The plant has deep, purple or white flowers. It is popularly used to make scent and perfume. Bathing in lavender water is considered to be soothing and refreshing. Acts as a substitute for perfume. Lavender scents are used as mental relaxants that raise the spirit. Lavender ointments are rubbed into burns, bruises, varicose veins and other skin injuries. The oil, when dabbed on, stops the itching of insect bites.

Lavender is one of the most popular ingredients for skin creams, lotions and hair conditioners.

- Lavender flowers can be soaked overnight in water. This can be used as a good body splash.

- A compound tincture of lavender can be used to relieve muscle spasms, nervousness and headaches. Rubbing a few drops of lavender oil on the temples cures a headache almost instantly.

- Lavender's essential oil is a potent ally in destroying a wide range of bacterial infections, pneumonia and flu viruses. It is also strongly anti-fungal.

- Lavender sachets kept between clothes and woollens is an effective insect-repellent that deters wool moths and mosquitoes.

Evening Primrose

This plant has fragrant, yellow flowers. It has elongated capsules filled with small, black seeds containing the oil. The entire evening primrose is edible. The roots are eaten, either pickled or boiled as vegetables. The young shoots can be added to salads.

It is an anti-coagulant. It reduces high-blood pressure, prevents heart attacks and guards against coronary artery disease.

Evening Primrose oil can be used on dry and flaky skin. It cures acne, eczema and improves blood circulation.

- The oil improves the condition of dry and brittle nails. It helps to moisten dry eyes.

- Evening Primrose gives relief to patients of rheumatoid arthritis.

- It helps the process of regeneration of liver cells, damaged by alcohol. It improves concentration of the mind.

- The herb prevents hangovers, post-drinking depression and alcohol withdrawal symptoms.

Parsley

Parsley *(ajmod)* is a very popular seasoning. It is used to garnish dishes and as an additive in pickles and salads.

Parsley contains Vitamin A and C, iron, manganese, calcium and phosphorus. It is high on protein. It is used in sauces, garnishes, tomato dishes, potatoes and peas.

The stems are used instead of leaves in making white sauces and stocks because they do not impart a green colour.

Fresh parsley is preferred in any dish but dried flakes can also be used in a pinch.

- Parsley leaves, seed and root are used in the treatment of urinary tract infections and help eliminate kidney stones.

- Parsley stimulates the appetite and increases blood flow to the digestive organs. It reduces fever and inflammation.

- A thick, green-yellow essential oil from parsley seeds is sometimes called "parsley camphor".

- It is also used to make creams effecting for bruises, hemorrhoids and varicose veins.

- This herb is popularly used to make scents, Oriental style perfumes and colognes.

Damask Rose

The Damask Rose is very beautiful and is used to adorn gardens and living rooms attractively. The flowers are a soft pink or red in colour. They are soft and very fragrant. Very graceful, they are the pride of a garden.

The damask rose is used for making *attar*. It contains Vitamin B, C, E and K. The rosehips and even the petals themselves make delicious jams, jellies, candies and syrups.

- Keep a bar of butter and rose petals in a closed jar overnight. By morning the butter gets a pleasing rose flavour. Spread the flavoured butter thinly over bread to make delicious sandwiches.

- Rose vinegar cures a sore throat and relieves headache.

- The leaves are a mild laxative. Rose oil is also antiseptic.

- Damask roses are a major source of *attar.* They are good for most skin types and used in a wide range of cosmetics.

- Mix one teaspoon of glycerine in two teaspoons each of lemon juice and rose water. Rub on face, neck, rough elbows and knees. It keeps the complexion soft and lovely. Cures dry, patchy skin.

Blackberry

Blackberry is popularly used to make pies, jams, jellies and all kinds of sweets. Blackberry wine and brandy are also very popular. It contains Vitamin C, organic acids and sugars.

Blackberry juice is an excellent astringent and cleanser.

- It is used as a remedy for diarrhoea.
- The root bark is a strong medicine. The gentler leaves are suggested for children.
- Blackberry syrup can be made from the extract of the roots and leaves.

Peppermint

It is a spreading, fragrant herb. The flowers are lilac pink on red, purple stems. Contains Vitamin A and C, calcium, potassium and menthol. Peppermint is a popular candy with children and leaves a refreshing taste in the mouth. It is the most widely used of all aromatic herbs. Peppermint's popular flavour is used in desserts, beverages, ice-cream, liquers, sauces, confectionaries, candies and a variety of after-dinner mints.

It cures indigestion and relaxes the muscles of the digestive tract. If peppermint is taken before eating, hunger pangs subside briefly, but soon return to increase the appetite. It relieves colon spasms, decreases inflammation and helps to heal ulcers.

Peppermint also eases nervous headaches, including migraine. Menthol, the main constituent of peppermint, helps kill bacteria, viruses and parasites in the stomach. It also destroys fungus infections, including ringworm and herpes simplex.

- Peppermint essential oil is used for flavouring chewing gum, candy and mints.

- Peppermint is widely used by aromatherapists. Peppermint scent increases concentration, stimulates the mind and body and keeps one awake.

- Make a strong tea using peppermint or add a few drops of its essential oil in a steaming pan of water. Inhale steam for a few minutes. Is very good for clearing stuffy nose and throat. Cleans blocked sinuses.

- Externally, the essential oil is used in balms and liniments as a combination cooling and heating agent that increases blood flow to the area.

Eucalyptus

This tall tree has a bluish, peeling bark, creamy flowers and leathery leaves. It is not a garden herb but it can be grown in pots. The gum or material that oozes from knots in eucalyptus trees is called kino and contains tannins.

Eucalyptus has been used for years, to cure fevers and as an antiseptic dressing on wounds and burns. Kino is used to treat dysentery. Small amounts of its essential oil are found in cough syrups and cough drops. Eucalyptol, derived from eucalyptus oil, is one of the main ingredients in Vicks Vapor Rub, which is rubbed on the chest during a cold. The oil is strongly antibiotic, destroying bacteria, fungi and viruses. It is used in the treatment of viral skin eruptions like herpes.

The leaves cool the body and reduce fever.

- Make a tea adding two teaspoons of dried eucalyptus leaves. Drink this for relief from bronchitis.

- Taking steam with a few drops of eucalyptus essential oil added to the water helps clear sinus and bronchial congestion.

- Eucalyptus oil is also used as a counter-irritant in liniments when rubbed on sore muscles or to heat rheumatism.

- Kino drinks are used as a tonic and as a mouthwash for toothache.

- The scent of eucalyptus is stimulating and keeps one awake and alert. It is found in aftershaves and colognes. It is used in cosmetic preparations to treat oily skin and acne.

Fennel

This herb contains Vitamin A and C, calcium, phosphorus and potassium. Fennel seeds *(saunf)* have a pleasing smell and flavour and are extensively used in cooking and also in ayurvedic medicines.

Fennel leaves are added to salads, sauces and soups and finely chopped to garnish sauces and puddings. It is used to flavour pickles and acts as a preservative.

Fennel seeds relax muscles, aid digestion and are particularly helpful in digesting fat. It is good for children's digestion. In fact, it is the main ingredient in gripewater, which is given to children when suffering from diarrhoea and indigestion.

- It is recommended for urinary tract inflammation and elimination of urinary stones.
- Fennel has been used as a popular weight-loss herb.
- Fennel is reported to be a mild stimulant and has the ability to increase milk production in nursing women.
- Fennel seeds, when boiled in water, make an excellent eyewash. They are said to improve eyesight. They are also reputed to reduce the effect of alcohol in the body.
- Fennel is used in facial steams, it cleanses pores and is used in anti-wrinkle creams. It is used to scent perfumes and soaps.

Licorice

This is a very popular herb in the making of confectionery and candies. It contains starch, sugar, amino acids, gums and essential oil.

Licorice *(Mulatthi)* flavours candies, liquers, ice-creams, chewing gum and baked foods. Its constituent "glycrrhizin" is fifty times sweeter than sugar. It is commonly chewed with betel leaves after meals.

This is good for the liver. It cures hormonal imbalances and peptic ulcers. It protects the spleen and the kidney. Licorice is recommended for neutralising toxins produced by diptheria, tetanus and intake of cocaine. It decreases inflammation and relieves arthritic and allergy symptoms.

Licorice reduces throat irritations, lung congestion and bacteria. It is used for coughs and bronchial problems.

Witch Hazel

Witch hazel is a small tree and looks attractive in gardens and can even be grown in pots. Its bright yellow and red leaves are striking in autumn.

Witch hazel water, lotion and ointment are easily available in drugstores.

It acts mostly on the veins and circulation. It has been shown to decrease the inflammation and pain of bruises, sore muscles, bleeding, hemorrhoids, varicose veins, nosebleeds and insect bites.

Witch hazel is antibacterial in nature. A weak tea of witch hazel serves as a good wash for inflamed eyes. It is a good astringent.

It lowers blood pressure and increases smoothness of respiration. It also relieves congestion. Witch Hazel is commonly used in aftershaves and mouthwashes. It is used in creams for treating pigmented skin. It clears blemishes.

Honeysuckle

This is a climbing shrub. Because of its elegance, it has a visual appeal. The flowers are fragrant, pale yellow or tinted pink.

Honeysuckle is used as a laxative. It increases sweating.

- A syrup made from the seeds and flowers of honeysuckle is good for liver and spleen problems, breathing problems, colds and flus.

- This herb has antibiotic properties. But it has poisonous berries.

- A honeysuckle wash is traditionally used to clear the complexion of freckles and sunburn.

Sweet Basil

Basil is regarded as royalty among all culinary herbs. Basil leaves accent any tomato dish and make delicious, herbal vinegar.

Basil leaves relieve indigestion and nausea and are effective even when there are side effects of chemotherapy. It is a gentle sedative for mild disorders.

Basil prevents peptic ulcers and other stress–related diseases like hypertension, colitis and asthma. Various species are used to treat colds and flus, to reduce fever, congestion and joint pain.

Basil has the ability to fight bacterial and fungal infections.

It is widely used in Ayurvedic medicines and is used to cure itching skin, ringworm, acne and poisonous insect bite.

- Sniffing the herb gets rid of headaches and lifts the spirits.

- Basil scent is used in soaps and cosmetics.

- Basil oil relieves tired muscles. Its fragrance decreases mental fatigue and clears the head. It restores the sense of smell, lost owing to sinus congestion.

Coriander

This green, leafy herb has a high content of Vitamin A and C, calcium, phosphorus and iron.

Probably one of the first cultivated spices, coriander has been in use as a spice and medicine for several centuries. It is a popular seasoning in vegetables and salads. It is commonly used to flavour cocktails and beverages. Coriander *(dhania)* seeds are used to make curries, breads and sauces.

Coriander seeds make laxatives taste better, especially bitter laxatives. They aid digestion, reduce gas and improve the appetite. The Chinese still use coriander tea to cure dysentery and measles. The oil is used as an antiseptic.

- Coriander seeds, mixed with lemon balm and water, make very good complexion water. It also provides raw material for the manufacture of synthetic perfume scents.

- The fragrance can also be used in soaps and natural deodorant.

- Coriander chutney is ideal to accompany rice, pulao and soups. Take six bunches of fresh coriander, a few cloves of garlic, one onion, a small piece of ginger and six green chillies. Add salt and a bit of sugar to taste. Mix in a blender and store in the refrigerator.

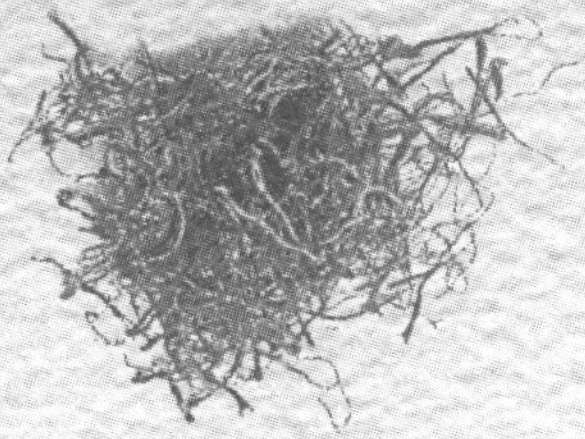

Saffron

This herb serves an ornamental purpose along with its medicinal and culinary uses. Saffron flowers are striking and fragrant, usually lilac or orange in colour. Bath water, laced with saffron extract, makes a refreshing and cleansing dip. Saffron *(kesar)* is a good stomach tonic, cures shortness of breath and depression. Its healing effect was recognised by people long ago. Small wonder that grandmothers still mix a few sprigs of saffron to hot milk and give their children. Saffron is used to flavour *kheer* and sweetmeats. It is also used in soups and salads. It is one of the most expensive spices in the world. It is good for the liver, heart and spleen.

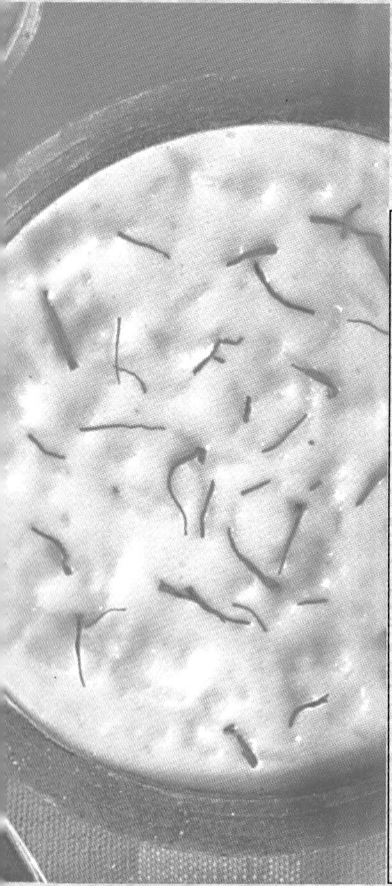

Saffron has a good aroma and adds a warm, spicy scent to perfumes.

- Saffron is a popular dye used to colour garments. In the medieval days, women dyed their hair with saffron.

- Use saffron in *suji halwa* and *kheer*. Apart from adding a pleasing colour, it also makes the dessert nutritious.